WET PUSSIES

Hilarious Snaps of Damp Cats

summersdale

CHARLIE ELLIS

WET PUSSIES

An Hachette UK Company
www.hachette.co.uk

Summersdale Publishers Ltd
Part of Octopus Publishing Group Limited
Carmelite House
50 Victoria Embankment
LONDON
EC4Y 0DZ
UK

www.summersdale.com

Printed and bound in China

ISBN: 978-1-80007-007-3

Substantial discounts on bulk quantities of Summersdale books are available to corporations, professional associations and other organizations. For details contact general enquiries: telephone: +44 (0) 1243 771107 or email: enquiries@summersdale.com.

To................................

From............................

Are you just gonna sit there and watch me get myself wet?

I WILL NOT BE THWARTED BY A NEMESIS SUCH AS YOU, SPRINKLER. I WILL CATCH THIS WATER!

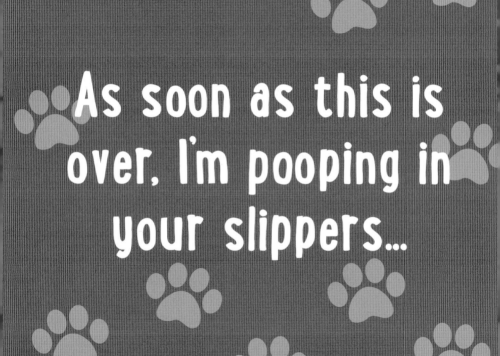

Oh, so I'm the only one not wearing a swimsuit?!

I AM AQUACAT. WELCOME TO MY WATERY REALM.

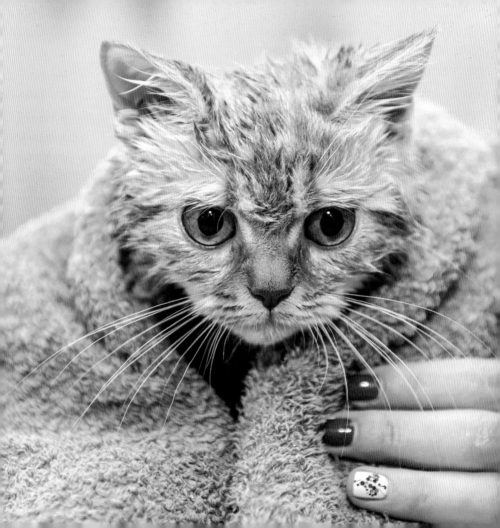

YES, THAT WAS A BIT OF A SHOCK, SUZIE. LET'S NEVER SPEAK OF IT AGAIN.

Soft, moist and furry.

YOU REALLY THOUGHT YOU COULD
GET THIS PUSSY SOAKING WET
AND I'D BE GRATEFUL?

That's rather a long rod. I wonder what comes out of it...

REALLY WORK THIS PUSSY WITH YOUR FINGERS.

I'm not getting back in that tub for all the kitty treats in the world!

YES, IT'S GUSHING.
COME FROLIC WITH ME.

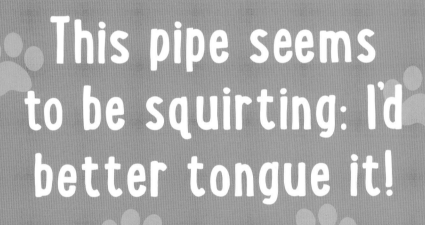
This pipe seems to be squirting: I'd better tongue it!

WE'RE NOT BFFS OR ANYTHING.
HE JUST LICKS ME DRY AFTER
I GO FOR MY SWIM.

If the fish won't come to Mr Whiskers, Mr Whiskers must come to the fish.

One more tummy rub, please.

Why would you bring me out to this lovely field to put me in a bubble bath?!

WHERE ARE YOUR
HANDS, SALLY, AND WHAT
ARE THEY DOING RIGHT NOW?

WELL, THAT'S AN EXPERIENCE I DON'T WANT TO REPEAT ANYTIME SOON. WHAT, WE HAVE TO DO THIS EVERY WEEK?!

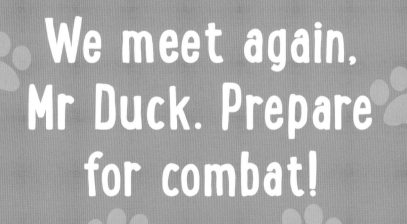
We meet again, Mr Duck. Prepare for combat!

EVER SEEN A PUSSY
THAT CAN LICK ITSELF?

Full wash and blow dry, please.

Don't you dare say this pussy looks more like a furious ball sack.

ACTUALLY, THAT BATH
WASN'T SO BAD. CAN'T BELIEVE
I'VE BEEN LICKING MYSELF
CLEAN ALL THESE YEARS.

IMAGE CREDITS

If you're interested in finding out more about our books, find us on Facebook at **Summersdale Publishers**, on Twitter at **@Summersdale** and on Instagram at **@summersdalebooks**.

www.summersdale.com